GREAT SPORTING EVENTS

Motorsports

Clive Gifford

FRANKLIN WATTS
LONDON · SYDNEY

Franklin Watts

First published in Great Britain in 2016 by The
Watts Publishing Group

Copyright © The Watts Publishing Group, 2016

Editors: Katie Dicker & Gerard Cheshire.
Art Direction: Cheena Yadav (Q2AMedia)
Designers: Kanika Kohli, Ravinder Kumar
(Q2AMedia)
Picture Researchers: Ankit Dubey, Sumedha
Chopra and Nivisha Sinha (Q2AMedia)

Picture credits:
t=top b=bottom c=centre l=left r=right

Front Cover: Jay LaPrete/AP Photo.
Back Cover: Ross Setford /NZPA/AP Photo,
Aijaz Rahi/AP Photo, Dave Thompson/AP Photo,
Mark J. Terrill/AP Photo, Jay LaPrete/AP Photo,
Anja Niedringhaus/AP Photo.
Title Page: David Vincent/AP Photo.
Imprint Page: Eckehard Schulz/AP Photo.
Insides: Eddie Worth/AP Photo: 4, Ong Chin
Kai/AP Photo: 5, Shuji Kajiyama/AP Photo: 6-7,
Mark Humphrey/AP Photo: 8, Mark Duncan/
AP Photo: 9, Rusty Kennedy/AP Photo: 10, Dale
Davis/AP Photo: 11, David Graham/AP Photo:
12, AP Photo: 13, David Vincent/AP Photo:
14-15, Wayne Drought/NZPA/AP Photo: 16,
Alastair Grant/AP Photo: 17, Natacha Pisarenko/
AP Photo: 18, Bernat Armangue/AP Photo: 19,
AP Photo: 20, Diego Azubel/AP Photo: 21, Gero
Breloer/AP Photo: 22, Paul Gilham/Getty Images
Sport/Getty Images: 23, Larry Lawrence/AMA
Pro Racing/AP Photo: 24, Luis M. Alvarez/AP
Photo: 25, Tom Hevezi/AP Photo: 26, Eckehard
Schulz/AP Photo: 27, Eddie Worth/AP Photo: 28.
Every attempt has been made to clear copyright.

Should there be any inadvertent omission, please
apply to the publisher for rectification.

ISBN: 978 1 4451 4963 9

Note: At the time of going to press, the statistics in this
book were up to date. However, due to the nature of
sport, it is possible that some of these may now be out
of date.

Printed in China

Franklin Watts
An imprint of
Hachette Children's Group
Part of The Watts Publishing Group
Carmelite House
50 Victoria Embankment
London EC4Y 0DZ

An Hachette UK Company
www.hachette.co.uk

www.franklinwatts.co.uk

MIX
Paper from
responsible sources
FSC® C104740

Contents

*Words in **bold** are in the glossary on page 30

High-speed races

Motor vehicles were invented and developed in the late 19th century. It wasn't long before they were raced against each other in exciting competitions. Today, motorsports fans flock to events in their thousands to watch races.

Fast action

The first ever motor race was from Paris to Rouen in France in 1894. It was completed at an average speed of 16.54km/h (10.28mph). Today's racing cars and motorcycles frequently race at speeds of over 300km/h (186.4mph).

On track

Motorsports events take place off-road or on track **circuits**. Many tracks are oval-shaped, with long straights and large 180° bends. Others, such as the Pocono Raceway in Pennsylvania, USA, are tri-ovals with three bends of 120° and three straights. Formula 1 cars (see pages 20–23) and some motorbikes also race on street circuits, which have lots of dramatic twists and turns.

Formula 1 cars **accelerate** at the start of a 1967 race at the famous Brands Hatch circuit in England.

All types

Whilst leading NASCAR (see pages 10–11) and Formula 1 (see pages 20–23) drivers are paid large sums of money to race, thousands of motorsports enthusiasts are **amateurs** who race for the thrill and the challenge. Almost all types of vehicle are raced in some sort of competition, from ride-on lawn mowers and school buses to the cabs of articulated trucks.

Start in karts

Karting is scaled-down racing in cars that sit very low to the ground. These are usually raced around small circuits with races lasting around 15 minutes. Many leading racing drivers, including Britain's Lewis Hamilton and Germany's Sebastian Vettel, began their careers in karting. At the highest level, Division 1 Superkarts are fearsome racing machines with top speeds of just over 250km/h (155mph).

Karts compete in the Singapore National Championship. The karts complete each lap of the course at an average speed of 80km/h (50mph).

GREAT SPORTING STATS

The fastest race vehicles of all are top fuel dragsters, which race in pairs along a straight track called a drag strip. In 2012, US dragster driver Spencer Massey reached a speed of 534.59km/h (332.18mph). His race on the 305-m long drag strip lasted about 3.8 seconds!

The IndyCar Series

Open-wheel racing features single-seater cars with drivers in open **cockpits**. They race around circuits made of smooth track. In North America, the most popular form of open-wheel racing is the IndyCar Series.

Long history, new start

For 30 years, there were two different competitions for US open-wheel racing, Indy Racing and CART or CHAMP cars. In 2008, these merged to form one competition, the IndyCar Series, run by the Indy Racing League. This organisation also runs the Indy Lights competition (with 16 races in 2015) for younger drivers.

Identical vehicles

Each IndyCar race team uses cars made from similar parts, which helps to make the races close and exciting. For instance, all the **chassis** are supplied by the same manufacturer and, in 2015, all the engines were either Honda or Chevrolet. The engines produce about four times as much power as a family car's engine and run on **ethanol**.

New Zealander Scott Dixon races his IndyCar around the Twin Ring Motegi circuit in Japan. His race vehicle can reach speeds of over 320km/h (199mph) on fast tracks.

Racing season

The IndyCar season begins in March and and usually runs until October. It comprises about 16 races. Races mostly take place in the USA, but have also been held in Canada, Brazil and Japan. They are mainly held in the afternoon on oval tracks, such as the Indianapolis Motor Speedway (see page 8), but the race calendar also includes some night races and some street circuit competitions, such as the Honda Indy Toronto in Canada and the Sao Paulo 300 in Brazil. For each race, teams adjust the **suspension** and **handling** of the cars to suit the circuit.

Points scoring

The race winner receives 50 points, second place 40 points and the points descend to five for each team sitting between 25th and 33rd in the race. In addition, the driver who leads the most laps receives two points and the **pole sitter** gets one point. In 2015, New Zealand driver Scott Dixon and Colombia's Juan Pablo Montoya were both leading with 556 points, but the IndyCar championship prize went to Dixon because he had won more races.

Danica Patrick, one of the most successful female racing drivers, shows off her trophy after winning the Indy Japan 300 in 2008.

GREAT SPORTING STATS

IndyCars usually race at top speeds of around 370km/h (230mph). The fastest recorded speed was in 1996 when Canada's Paul Tracy drove his car at 413.52km/h (256.9mph) at the Michigan International Speedway, USA.

Indianapolis 500

The Indy 500 is IndyCar's most famous race and one of the most prestigious races in the world. Held since 1911 at the Indianapolis Motor Speedway in the USA, an estimated audience of 400,000 race fans attend the race weekend at the end of May.

The Brickyard

Built in 1908, the 4.02km (2.5 miles) oval track was originally made from crushed rock and tar, which proved dangerous as ruts and holes formed and loose stones would fly up and hit drivers. It was then covered in 3.2 million bricks set in sand to provide a new racing surface, earning it the nickname 'The Brickyard'. The bricks are now covered in a layer of **asphalt**, but nine rows remain exposed at the finish line. Winners of the Indy 500 often kiss the bricks after getting out of their cars.

Pole sitter Helio Castroneves leads at the 2009 Indy 500, so named as it covers 500 miles (805km).

Qualifying and bumping

Drivers complete four-lap time trials to **qualify** for the race on the weekend preceding the race weekend. On the Saturday, known as Pole Day, the fastest drivers win positions 1–24 in the 33-car race, with the fastest being made the pole sitter. On the Sunday, time trials continue and the fastest drivers win the remaining nine positions. Any of the Sunday drivers whose time trial is faster than one achieved by the fastest drivers on the Saturday 'bumps' that driver out of their qualifying position.

Race champions

Three American racing greats, Rick Mears, A J Foyt and Al Unser, have all won the Indy 500 four times. Unser is part of a great racing family. His brother Bobby won three Indy 500s and his son, Al Unser Jr, won the race twice. In recent years, champions have come from as far afield as Britain, Brazil and New Zealand.

GREAT SPORTING STATS

During the 1996 Indy 500, Eddie Cheever completed a lap at 379.9km/h (236mph) — the fastest race lap ever. Sarah Fisher completed a 2002 qualifying lap of the Indy 500 at an average speed of 369km/h (229mph) — the fastest by a female driver.

Rick Mears celebrates his fourth Indy 500 in 1991. The Borg-Warner Trophy features the sculptured faces of more than 90 winners of the race. Winners traditionally celebrate by drinking a bottle of milk.

NASCAR

The National Association for **Stock Car** Auto Racing (NASCAR) is the leading stock car association in the world. It was formed by race driver and promoter Bill France Senior in 1948. Since that time, it has become the USA's most popular form of car racing.

The Sprint Cup

NASCAR runs a large range of competitions, including races for pick-up trucks and up-and-coming drivers. Its leading competition, however, is the Sprint Cup. This competition is watched by millions of people over its 36 races. It begins in February and ends in November.

The cars

The cars used in Sprint Cup racing are stripped-down vehicles with steel panelled bodies, few electronic aids and no wing mirrors. They have sturdy roll-cages to protect the drivers and enormously powerful engines, which can take cars to speeds of over 310km/h (192.6mph).

US driver Greg Sacks' NASCAR vehicle goes flying through the air after a high speed crash during the AC Spark Plug 500 NASCAR race.

Close racing

Qualifying takes place on the Friday before the race. It is based on the drivers' fastest times over two laps and determines the order in which drivers take up their starting positions. A maximum **field** of 43 cars is allowed in a Sprint Cup race. This can lead to incredibly tight racing, with frequent shunts and some crashes during the three to four hours it takes to complete an 805km (500 mile) race.

Chase for the championship

In 2011 the racing points system was simplified. A race victory is now awarded 43 points, plus three bonus points for winning and a bonus point for leading a lap (to a maximum of 48 points). Second place gets 42 points, plus any bonus points for leading a lap or a bonus point for leading the most laps, and so on down to the final finisher, who receives one point.

Jimmie Johnson, in car No 48, leads during the Aaron's 499 NASCAR race at the Talladega Superspeedway in 2010.

GREAT SPORTING STATS

One closely-watched NASCAR statistic is the number of changes of race leader in a race. In the 2011 Sprint Cup, there was an average of 27.1 lead changes per race and an average of 12.8 leaders per race — two new NASCAR records.

Daytona 500

NASCAR's Sprint Cup includes the Daytona 500, a 500 mile-long race over 200 laps of the Daytona International Speedway, in Florida, USA. The winner receives over US$1.5 million (£1 million) and a replica of the famous Harley J. Earl Trophy.

A crowd of many thousands at the Daytona International Speedway track watch the Daytona 500.

Daytona International Speedway

The Daytona International Speedway is the venue for Superbike motorcycle racing, and a 24-hour **endurance** race, as well as the Daytona 500. Inside the tri-oval track is a lake, Lake Lloyd, and seating for around 125,000 race fans.

Start of the season

The Daytona 500 is held in February and is the very first points-scoring race of the NASCAR season. Qualifying occurs the weekend before to determine the order of the 43 cars in the big race.

An open race

Qualifying in pole position is no guarantee of success – only nine pole sitters have won in 57 races. Exciting overtaking, crashes and changes of lead are commonplace. In 2009, for example, Matt Kenseth started the race in 43rd place and went on to win.

Close finishes

The first Daytona 500, in 1959, ended in a **photo finish** as two cars crossed the line at almost the same time. The winner was Lee Petty, the father of NASCAR legend Richard Petty (see panel). Other close finishes include the 2007 race where Kevin Harvick beat Mark Martin by a tiny margin of just 0.02 seconds.

GREAT SPORTING STATS

The great Richard Petty (NASCAR career: 1958–1992) is one of NASCAR's all-time leading drivers. 'The King', as he was nicknamed, won 200 NASCAR races including a record seven Daytona 500 victories. Only eight times has the winner of the Daytona 500 gone on to win the entire NASCAR championship. Richard Petty achieved this feat four times.

Richard Petty speeds round the Daytona track during practice for the 1968 Daytona 500. Petty won Daytona 500 races in the 1960s, 1970s and 1980s.

Le Mans 24 Hours

Endurance races last many hours. The most famous of all is the Le Mans 24 Hours race in France. Teams of three relaying drivers, with one car, race for an entire 24 hours non-stop. The winning team is the one that covers the greatest distance in that time.

During the Le Mans 24 Hours race, drivers use headlamps to race through the night.

Circuit de la Sarthe

The Le Mans race was first held on the historic Circuit de la Sarthe, back in 1923. Over the years, it has undergone many changes and is now 13.65km (8.48 miles) long. One of its most famous features is the Mulsanne Straight where speeds can exceed 300km/h (186mph), before heavy braking gets cars down to 50–70km/h (31–43mph) so that they can travel through the tight Mulsanne Corner without leaving the track.

Race start

Around 50 cars take part in Le Mans, which is held in June each year. In 2015, the race was watched by 263,500 spectators. Up until 1970, the drivers ran from one side of the track and jumped into their cars to start the race. Now, drivers begin with a **rolling start** in the afternoon and race through the night and into the next day.

Teams and stops

In 1984, Germany's Klaus Ludwig and France's Henri Pescarolo became the last two-driver team to win Le Mans. All cars now have three drivers, none of whom can drive for more than four hours at a time. Swapping drivers, refuelling, fitting new tyres and running repairs mean that cars make a number of **pit stops** throughout the race.

Le Mans legends

Some drivers love Le Mans. Henri Pescarolo from France has raced there a record 33 times, winning four times. Denmark's Tom Kristensen holds the record for most wins with nine; in 1997, 2008 and 2013 and a run of six in a row 2000–2005. Seven of his nine wins came in Audi cars. The other two wins were in a Bentley and a Porsche. Porsche remains the leading make of car, with 16 Le Mans wins.

Tom Kristensen raises his hand in celebration as he crosses the finish line to win the Le Mans race in 2008.

GREAT SPORTING STATS

The 2010 Le Mans winners – Germany's Mike Rockenfeller and Timo Bernhard and France's Romain Dumas completed 397 laps of the track as they covered a distance of around 5,410km (3,361.6 miles). This works out at an average speed of over 225km/h (140mph).

World Rally Championship

In rally races, cars race on-road and off-road over a series of timed stages. The peak of rallying is the World Rally Championship (WRC). Hugely popular, crowds of over half a million people can gather to watch the various stages of a WRC rally.

Rally calendar

The WRC competition began in 1973. Over the years, the number of rallies held each season has changed. In 2015, the competition featured 13 races from January to November.

In between, teams travel the world to compete in rallies in countries such as Jordan, Japan, Mexico and New Zealand. The remaining rallies are all held in Europe.

Norway's Henning Solberg takes to the air as he negotiates a narrow bridge during Rally New Zealand.

Rally stages

Each rally lasts three days and is divided into 15–25 stages, with a typical day's racing covering 400km (248.5 miles). The various stages of each race may be on different surfaces, from loose sand and gravel to ice and snow. These offer different challenges to the skills and reactions of the driver and **co-driver** or navigator.

Championship points

Cars race against the clock, trying to record quicker times than their rivals. The winner of a rally scores 25 points, with second place awarded 18 points. The following eight cars score points from 15 down to one. These points count towards the drivers' championship. A driver may race alone or as part of a team. Points won by a team's top two cars count towards the manufacturers' championship.

GREAT SPORTING STATS

Sébastien Loeb has an incredible World Rally Championship record. The French driver has won 78 WRC rallies and finished in the top three 38 more times. These victories have propelled Loeb to a record nine championships in a row (2004–2012).

Sébastien Loeb (right), of France, and co-driver Daniel Elena, of Monte Carlo, celebrate with the WRC Drivers' Championship trophy.

The Dakar Rally

First held in late 1978 and early 1979, the Dakar Rally is the ultimate long-distance motorsports event. Every year, cars, motorbikes, quadbikes and trucks race for over two weeks across more than 9,000km (5,592 miles) of challenging, tough terrain.

France's David Fretigne tackles the desert terrain in the 2010 Dakar Rally.

The rally route

Traditionally, the race began in Paris and ended in the Senegal city of Dakar. In 1977, French motorcycle racer, Thierry Sabine, got lost in the African desert during the Abidjan-Nice rally. He decided to create an epic long-distance race from his home country, France, through the desert.

However, this route has been altered a number of times. For example, in 1995 it began in the Spanish city of Grenada, and in 2009, after security worries in Africa, the entire rally was moved to South America where it has been held ever since.

Racing classes

Every year there are several winners of the Dakar Rally because there are separate competition classes for cars, trucks, motorbikes and quadbikes. The 2015 Rally finishers featured 67 cars, 43 trucks, 79 motorbikes and 18 quadbikes. In 1992, Ethiopia's Hubert Auriol became the first person to win the Dakar both in a car (1992) and on a motorbike (1981/1983).

Strenuous stages

The rally is split up into a series of stages, mostly over distances of between 200–600km (125–370 miles). The racing is a real test of endurance over many days, not only for the drivers but also the vehicles, which have to deal with all sorts of conditions from rocky plains to mud and sand dunes. Since 2014, motorbikes and quadbikes have completed a different route to cars and trucks.

Dakar legends

In 2001, Germany's Jutta Kleinschmidt became the first woman to win the Dakar Rally. Twelve years later, France's Stéphane Peterhansel won his fifth Dakar Rally in a car. This was in addition to his astonishing six wins in the motorcycle class.

German driver Jutta Kleinschmidt and her co-driver Fabrizio Pons, from Italy, **navigate** the desert dunes during the first stage of the Dakar Rally.

GREAT SPORTING STATS

In the Dakar Rally, trucks are classed as vehicles weighing more than 3,500kg. The Kamaz racing team from Russia has the best record in the truck racing category of the Dakar Rally, having won 13 rallies in total.

Formula 1

Formula 1 (F1) cars are highly advanced, open-wheel racing cars that cost tens of millions of pounds to develop. They feature in a worldwide championship of Grand Prix races – the most popular motorsports competition in the world.

Cream of the crop

Racing drivers all over the world start out with the dream of racing in Formula 1. There are many levels of racing below F1, with GP2 considered to be the competition just one step below Formula 1. Success in that competition can lead to being offered a place in a Formula 1 team. British driver Lewis Hamilton, for example, became GP2 champion in 2006 and moved up to F1 the following year.

Around the world

In the first Formula 1 season in 1950, there were just seven races. Recent seasons have featured 18 or 19 races, with the season beginning in March and ending in November. In between, F1 teams travel to Australia, Japan, Canada, China and many other countries. Teams develop and refine their technology throughout a race season and drivers often have to adapt to new versions of their cars.

Lorenzo Bandini of Italy races in his Ferrari Formula 1 car at the 1966 United States Grand Prix.

Britain's Lewis Hamilton makes a pit stop in his McLaren Mercedes car during the 2009 Chinese Grand Prix. Pit teams can refuel a car in under six seconds.

Grand Prix races

The week of a Formula 1 race begins with practice sessions and then qualifying, usually the day before the race, to determine each car's position on the **starting grid**. Races are around 305km (190 miles) long and are completed in around 90 minutes of intense racing. Cars can accelerate from a standstill to 160km/h (100mph) in just 3.5 seconds, and can reach top speeds of 340km/h (211mph).

Rule changes

Changes to the racing rules occur frequently in Formula 1. In 2015, for example, the minimum weight for each car was increased so that taller (or heavier) drivers were not penalised.

GREAT SPORTING STATS

In 2010, a new points system for Formula 1 was introduced, with cars finishing from first to tenth place gaining points. Here are the new points for places with the previous points system in brackets.

1st 25 (10)
2nd 18 (8)
3rd 15 (6)
4th 12 (5)
5th 10 (4)
6th 8 (3)
7th 6 (2)
8th 4 (1)
9th 2 (0)
10th 1 (0)

Famous F1 races and drivers

Points in each F1 race count towards two separate competitions – the Drivers' Championship for individual racers and the Constructors' Championship for the race teams they drive for. In 2015, Lewis Hamilton won the drivers' crown and his team, Mercedes, the constructors' title.

Lewis Hamilton raises the trophy after winning the 2015 British F1 Grand Prix at Silverstone.

Championship winners

Ferrari has been the most successful team in Formula 1, having taken part since it began in 1950, and winning over 220 races and 15 Constructors' Championships. Germany's Michael Schumacher with an astonishing 91 Formula 1 race wins and seven Drivers' Championships is the most successful F1 driver of all time.

Different circuits

Part of Formula 1's appeal is how the race circuits differ greatly from one another. Some, such as Monaco and the Singapore Grand Prix tracks, run through city streets. Others are on permanent dedicated race circuits, such as Hockenheim in Germany and Monza in Italy.

The Monaco Grand Prix circuit is a thrilling ride, with many twists and hairpin bends.

The Monaco Grand Prix

First held in 1929, the Monaco Grand Prix is one of the highlights of Formula 1's year. The race is held on Monaco's public roads, which are converted every year into a twisting, turning 3.34km (2 mile) circuit. It is one of the toughest tests of a driver's skills, with hundreds of sharp changes in speed and tight bends requiring over 4,000 gear changes during the 78-lap race.

Sebastian Vettel was 21 when he won the Italian Grand Prix in 2008 and became the youngest ever race winner. Two years later, he won his first Formula 1 World Championship. By 2013, he had become the youngest ever four-time world champion.

Triple crown

The Monaco Grand Prix, along with the Indianapolis 500 and the Le Mans 24 Hours race, are known as motorsports' triple crown. Only one man has won all three events – Britain's Graham Hill, in the 1960s and 70s.

Motocross championships

Motocross is an exciting motorcycle sport that begins when up to 40 riders gather for a massed start. They race a number of laps of a closed off-road style circuit, complete with dips, bumps, hills and jumps. The aim is to cross the finish line first to gain maximum points.

Tough racing

Top level motocross races last around 30–40 minutes and place enormous strains on a rider's strength and reactions. Close racing and the obstacles on the course often take their toll and crashes and falls are common. Riders are protected with a full-face helmet and padded racing leathers.

Motocross bikes

Motocross bikes are light but sturdily built, with long saddles for riders to shift their weight around as they jump, land and throw their bikes into tight bends. Bikes race in different classes based on their engine sizes and capacities. The 125cc and 250cc classes are the most popular.

US motocross star Jeremy Martin takes part in the 2014 AMA 250 Class Motocross Championship.

AMA Motocross Championship

Motocross is run by a number of organisations. In the USA, the American Motorcyclist Association (**AMA**) is the leading body. Its championship is held between May and September over 12 different race days, each featuring two races with 25 points on offer for each race win. In 2015, the AMA 250 Class competition was won by Jeremy Martin, scoring 491 points.

The World Motocross Championship

In the rest of the world, the **FIM** (Fédération Internationale de Motocyclisme) runs a major motocross competition with up to 18 different race days, each with two races. Most circuits are in Europe, but occasionally races are held in South America, the Middle East and Asia. Since 2005, a Women's World Motocross Championship has been run. Italy's Kiara Fontanesi was champion four times between 2012 and 2015.

GREAT SPORTING STATS

US rider Ricky Carmichael, nicknamed GOAT (Greatest Of All Time), was undefeated across the entire AMA Motocross season in 2002, 2004 and 2005.

Motocross legend Ricky Carmichael makes a flying jump on his bike during a Supercross series race in Florida, USA.

MotoGP

A motorcycling world championship was first held in 1949. In 2002 the 500cc motorbike class was renamed MotoGP with the introduction of 990cc engines. In 2012, the engine capacity was raised to 1,000cc.

Monster motorbikes

MotoGP motorbikes are extremely powerful machines. They are built by major motorcycle manufacturers and are not available for sale to the public. No expense is spared in constructing these incredibly powerful bikes. In 2015 at the Qatar Grand Prix, Spanish MotoGP rider Marc Márquez reached a record speed of 350.5km/h (217.8mph) on his Honda RC213V motorbike.

MotoGP season

A MotoGP season begins in April with the Qatar Grand Prix in the Middle East. The competition lasts 18 rounds and is held in 14–16 different countries, including Australia, Japan, Spain, Malaysia and the UK. Races vary in length, but usually take around 45 minutes, in which riders complete around 35 laps of a track.

Spain's Jorge Lorenzo leads a pack of MotoGP riders through a turn at the British Grand Prix at Donington circuit.

Italy's Valentino Rossi has an incredible record in motorcycle racing. In over 230 races, he has recorded 73 race wins. He has also finished in second or third place 79 times. Rossi has won the MotoGP World Championship on seven occasions (2001, 2002, 2003, 2004, 2005, 2008 and 2009).

Italy's Valentino Rossi reacts after winning the MotoGP race of the German Motorcycle Grand Prix, 2009.

Points winners

A MotoGP race winner receives 25 points, second place 20, third place 16, fourth place 13, down to 15th place with one point. Over a season, a top rider strives to not only win races but also to make sure that they gain points in the races they don't win. In 2009, Italian racer Valentino Rossi won six races but also finished second, third or fourth an impressive eight times to win his seventh MotoGP World Championship.

1894 The first organised motor race occurs; a city-to-city race between Paris and Rouen.

1906 The first major Italian road race, the Targa Florio, is run.

1911 The first Indy 500 race.

1923 The first running of Le Mans 24 Hours.

1927 Opening of the legendary Nordschleife track at the Nürburgring in Germany.

1929 The first Monaco Grand Prix.

1950 The first Formula 1 Grand Prix championship season.

1950 NASCAR's first 500-mile race, the Southern 500, is held.

1957 Argentina's Juan Manuel Fangio becomes the oldest ever F1 world champion at the age of 47.

1958 US driver Richard Petty enters NASCAR for the first time. He goes on to win 200 races.

1959 The Daytona International Speedway is opened.

1966 Italy's Giacomo Agostini wins the first of eight Grand Prix motorcycling world championships.

1972 The first stadium motocross event held in Los Angeles, USA.

1972 Britain's Graham Hill becomes the first to win the Indy 500, the Formula 1 World Championship and the Le Mans 24 Hours.

1973 The World Rally Championship begins.

1975 Italy's Lella Lombardi becomes the first female driver to win Formula 1 championship points, coming sixth in the Spanish Grand Prix.

1978 The first running of the Paris-Dakar Rally, later known as the Dakar Rally.

1981 France's Michele Mouton becomes the first woman to win a World Rally Championship event, the Sanremo rally.

1987 The Suzuka circuit in Japan becomes a Formula 1 race for the first time.

1999 Finland's Tommi Mäkinen becomes the first driver to win the World Rally Championship four times in a row.

2001 Germany's Jutta Kleinschmidt becomes the first woman to win the Dakar Rally.

2002 The MotoGP competition begins, replacing the 500cc Grand Prix.

2008 Danica Patrick, of the USA, becomes the first woman to win an IndyCar race.

2013 Germany's Sebastian Vettel wins his fourth Formula 1 World Championship.

2013 Jimmie Johnson adds another NASCAR championship to his record five-in-a-row run from 2006–10.

Formula 1 cars racing in the 1960s.

Winner tables

Formula 1 Championship

Year	Driver	Team
2015	Lewis Hamilton (Britain)	Mercedes (Germany)
2014	Lewis Hamilton (Britain)	Mercedes (Germany)
2013	Sebastian Vettel (Germany)	Red Bull (Austria)
2012	Sebastian Vettel (Germany)	Red Bull (Austria)
2011	Sebastian Vettel (Germany)	Red Bull (Austria)
2010	Sebastian Vettel (Germany)	Red Bull (Austria)
2009	Jenson Button (Britain)	Brawn (Britain)
2008	Lewis Hamilton (Britain)	McLaren (Britain)

NASCAR Nextel/Sprint Cup

Year	Driver	Vehicle make
2015	Kyle Busch	Toyota
2014	Kevin Harvick	Chevrolet
2013	Jimmie Johnson	Chevrolet
2012	Brad Keselowski	Dodge
2011	Tony Stewart	Chevrolet
2010	Jimmie Johnson	Chevrolet
2009	Jimmie Johnson	Chevrolet
2008	Jimmie Johnson	Chevrolet
2007	Jimmie Johnson	Chevrolet
2006	Jimmie Johnson	Chevrolet
2005	Tony Stewart	Chevrolet

World Rally Championship

Year	Champion driver	Champion manufacturer
2015	Sébastien Ogier (France)	Volkswagen
2014	Sébastien Ogier (France)	Volkswagen
2013	Sébastien Ogier (France)	Volkswagen
2012	Sébastien Loeb (France)	Citroën
2011	Sébastien Loeb (France)	Citroën
2010	Sébastien Loeb (France)	Citroën
2009	Sébastien Loeb (France)	Citroën
2008	Sébastien Loeb (France)	Citroën
2007	Sébastien Loeb (France)	Citroën
2006	Sébastien Loeb (France)	Citroën
2005	Sébastien Loeb (France)	Citroën

MotoGP

Year	Champion rider	Champion vehicle
2015	Jorge Lorenzo (Spain)	Yamaha
2014	Marc Márquez (Spain)	Honda
2013	Marc Márquez (Spain)	Honda
2012	Jorge Lorenzo (Spain)	Yamaha
2011	Casey Stoner (Australia)	Honda
2010	Jorge Lorenzo (Spain)	Yamaha
2009	Valentino Rossi (Italy)	Yamaha
2008	Valentino Rossi (Italy)	Yamaha
2007	Casey Stoner (Australia)	Ducati
2006	Nicky Hayden (USA)	Honda
2005	Valentino Rossi (Italy)	Yamaha

Glossary and further info

Accelerate To increase speed.

AMA Short for the American Motorcyclist Association, the body which organises and promotes the leading motorcycle racing competitions in the USA.

Amateur A driver, rider or team not paid to take part in motorsports competitions.

Asphalt A sticky oil-based substance, used to provide a smooth and hardwearing top surface on tracks and roads.

Chassis The base frame of a car.

Circuit Another name for tracks used in car and motorcycle racing events.

Cockpit The space in a car for the driver.

Co-driver The navigator in a rally, who gives the driver course instructions as they race.

Endurance To be able to do something for a long period of time.

Ethanol A type of fuel made from alcohol.

Field The number of vehicles in a motor race.

FIM Short for *Fédération Internationale de Motocyclisme,* the body which runs many leading world motorcycling competitions.

Handling How a car responds when racing, changing speeds and altering direction.

Navigate In rallying, to plot a route from one place to another.

Open-wheel Types of racing cars, usually single-seater vehicles, with their wheels outside of their bodies.

Photo finish When two or more competitors in a race cross the finishing line at the same time, a photo is used to tell who the winner is.

Pit stop When a car or bike leaves the racetrack and enters a pit area to receive fuel, tyre changes or repairs.

Pole sitter (also known as pole position) The driver with the best position at the front of a starting grid, because his car or bike has qualified with the fastest time.

Qualifying Races or timed sessions that decide the order of the starting grid at the beginning of a race.

Rolling start When race vehicles perform preliminary laps of the track and are on the move as the race starts.

Starting grid The area of the track where cars line up just before a race starts.

Stock car A form of motor racing on tracks using modified versions of cars produced for sale to the public.

Suspension The system of springs, shock absorbers and other parts which are joined to the wheels or axles and affect how a car or bike handles.

Websites

http://www.autoracing1.com
An American motorsports website with news on major competitions including NASCAR, Formula 1 and IndyCar racing.

http://www.crash.net
This website carries in-depth news and details of Formula 1 and MotoGP racing, as well as other classes of motorsport.

http://www.motorsport.com
This comprehensive website features competition news, race dates and the results of major events from the Dakar Rally to Indycars.

http://www.fia.com
The official website of the Fédération Internationale de l'Automobile, the organisation which runs world motorsports.

http://www.fim-live.com/en
The FIM runs many of the world's major motorcycling racing competitions including Enduro and MotoGP.

http://www.formula1.com
Formula 1's official website is full of in-depth features on the drivers, teams, the technology and guides to the race circuits.

http://www.nascar.com
The official NASCAR racing website has pages filled with information on teams, drivers, races and technology.

http://www.wrc.com/index.jsp
The official website of the World Rally Championship, with a complete schedule of the current season, driver profiles, photos and video footage.

http://www.motogp.com
The official MotoGP website includes news, exciting photos and videos of race action.

http://www.ama-cycle.org
The home of the American Motorcyclist Association (AMA)'s racing division, including links to motocross and other competitions.

http://www.planetlemans.com
This website focuses on the Le Mans 24 Hours competition as well as other forms of endurance racing.

http://www.dakar.com
The official website of the Dakar Rally is packed with profiles of leading drivers and detailed course maps.

http://www.indycar.com
The official website of the IndyCar Series has full details of races, results and video clips.

http://www.rallye-info.com/Default.asp
Use this website to keep up-to-date with all the latest news in rally racing.

Further reading

EDGE: The Inside Track: Lewis Hamilton vs Nico Rosberg – Paul Mason (Franklin Watts, 2016)
An exciting, high-octane account of a classic F1 race

Motorsports – Clive Gifford (Franklin Watts, 2009)
A series of books all about the fast world of motorsport

Index